ALSO BY ANITA DIAMANT

The New Jewish Wedding
The Jewish Baby Book

What to Name

Anita Diamant

Your Jewish Baby

SUMMIT BOOKS

NEW YORK • LONDON • TORONTO • SYDNEY • TOKYO

SUMMIT BOOKS
Simon & Schuster Building
Rockefeller Center
1230 Avenue of the Americas
New York, New York 10020

Copyright © 1989 by Anita Diamant
All rights reserved
including the right of reproduction
in whole or in part in any form.
SUMMIT BOOKS and colophon are
trademarks of Simon & Schuster Inc.
Designed by Edith Fowler
Manufactured in the United States of America

10 9 8 7 6 5 4 3 2 1

Library of Congress Cataloging in Publication Data
Diamant, Anita.
    What to name your Jewish baby / Anita Diamant.
        p.   cm.
    1. Names, Personal—Jewish—Dictionaries.   I. Title.
CS3010.D53   1989
929.4′4′089924—dc20   89-21571
                                                           CIP

ISBN 0-671-68866-9

IN MEMORY OF MY GRANDPARENTS,
ESTHER LEAH AND ABRAHAM,
ESTHER MALKAH AND DAVID MORDECHAI

Contents

"With each child, the world begins anew."
                                    —THE MIDRASH

Acknowledgments

Thanks to the following people for their insights about the Jewish way of naming, and for help in compiling the list: Rabbi Ramie Arian, Jim Ball, Shula Braun, Howard Cooper, Rabbi Neal Cooper, Orli Kalchouk, Rabbi Lawrence Kushner, Rabbi Barbara Penzner, Arthur Samuelson, Frieda Shapira, Rabbi Rifat Soncino, Ella Taylor, Moshe Waldoks.

✤ Introduction

FEW PARENTS approach the subject of their child's name with indifference. Some people have names selected before they conceive. Some couples spend the nine months of pregnancy poring over lists and ask friends and relatives for feedback on the top contenders. Others wait until after the baby is born before settling on what to call him or her. Some couples keep the names they select for their child a secret and others refer to the mother's belly by its soon-to-be name.

However you go about it, choosing your baby's name is a second conception. Like Adam's appointed task of giving names to all living things in Eden, naming is an exercise of power and creativity.

What to Name Your Jewish Baby is different from all the other name books available. This book begins with the fact that you are interested in grounding your choice in the religious, historical, and cultural context of Judaism. You have decided to focus your options—indeed narrow them—in order to express your child's and your family's connection to the Jewish tradition.

For Jews, a name is a complicated gift. It bestows not only identity but also a living connection to previous generations. Indeed, every

Jew's name acknowledges his or her parents' names. On official documents, a boy named Michael is known as Michael, the son of his father Mark and his mother Anne—*Michael bar Moshe v' Hasida.* Likewise, Hannah is *Hanna bat Chaim v' Zahavah,* Hanna, the daughter of Howard and Janet.[1]

And because Jews usually give names to honor the memory of people who have died, they are also living testimonials to grandparents and great-grandparents. Furthermore, your infant Daniel or Rebecca is the latest link in a continuous chain back to the first biblical Daniel and Rebecca.

Giving a Jewish name is an opportunity to express family pride, historic consciousness, religious concerns, and spiritual aspirations. Naming is an act of faith and hope that your children will remember the meaning of their names and the lives of their namesakes; and that their lives will add another generation of honor to the names they bear.

Which is why *What to Name Your Jewish Baby* is more than just a list of names. It contains information about the rich cultural heritage—the history, customs, even some of the superstitions—associated with Jewish names. However, it is important to remember that there is almost no *halachah,* or Jewish law, regarding the choice of names. Even the most widespread practices, such as naming children after relatives, are not written in stone. And no matter what expectant grandparents insist is the one-and-only "correct" way to name a Jewish baby, customs are not written in stone; they vary from one culture to the next, and change over time.

The names in this book do not comprise a definitive dictionary or a scholarly collection. This list reflects the author's best efforts to find Hebrew, Yiddish, Sephardic, and English names with a Jewish pedigree—names that American parents might realistically choose for children living and going to school in an English-speaking country in the 1990s. Hopefully, among the familiar and exotic, the ancient and brand-new names compiled here, you will find the perfect name for your wonderful baby. If you need further help or guidance, rabbis, cantors, *mohels*, and native Hebrew-speakers can be invaluable resources.

One reason that Jews name their babies after loved ones derives from the idea that the name of a person who lives an exemplary life—a life filled with good works, study, and love—is itself a blessing. Selecting a name is the first decision Jewish parents make for their children.* It is the beginning of the process of shaping the exemplary person—the *mensch*—your child can be.

---

*The next choices for Jews revolve around the rituals that welcome new babies into the covenant of the people of Israel—into the Jewish community. For a complete guide to circumcision *(brit milah)*, covenant ceremonies for daughters *(brit habat)*, adoption ceremonies and more, see *The Jewish Baby Book* by Anita Diamant (Summit Books, 1988).

🌿 A Jewish Name

IN CULTURES around the world and throughout history, names have been powerful magic. *HaShem*, The Name, is one of the most common ways Jews refer to God. Not only is God's real name unpronounceable, The Name is unknowable because there is a sense in which it is more than just symbol or signifier. The Name mysteriously contains the essence, power, and unity that is God.

Israel ben Eliezer, the founder of the eighteenth century mystical revival movement called Hasidism, was called the Baal Shem Tov, the Master of the Good Name. That title not only reflected his own reputation for goodness, but also suggested that he knew more about the power and wisdom of The Name than most.

The Bible portrays naming as the first independent human act. Adam's job in Eden was to name the beasts of the field and the birds of the air and every living thing. This was no make-work project. The Hebrew for "word," *davar*, is also the Hebrew for "thing." Thus, the name and the essence of temporal things are, in some fundamental way, the same. There is something about human names that

18

confirms this insight. A woman named Rose, by any other name, would somehow be someone other than Rose. Rose is Rose, just as Esther is, unalterably, Esther.

The Torah underscores the importance of names in its attention to dramatic name changes. Once they enter into a covenant with God, Abram and Sarai become different people—Abraham and Sarah—the parents of the Jewish people. And Jacob, "supplanter," after struggling with the angel, is renamed Israel, "wrestler with God," and becomes the patriarch of the twelve tribes.

Acknowledging the importance of naming, the Midrash advises, "One should examine names carefully in order to give his son a name that is worthy so that the son may become a righteous person, for sometimes the name is a contributing factor for good as for evil." And Proverb 22 says, "A good name is rather to be chosen than good oil." Oil was a measure of wealth and "a good name" probably refers to reputation. But the sense that names contain an inherent value and power is strong in Jewish tradition. According to rabbinic tradition, the Hebrews became lax in their faith during their enslavement in Egypt, but they were saved from total assimilation by holding fast to two customs that set them apart: circumcision and their distinctive Hebrew names.

But, above all, Jewish tradition stresses that a good name is earned, and the power attributed to a generically "good" name is really only as strong as the person who bears it. The Mishnah says, "The crown of a good name excels all other crowns, including the crown of learning, of priesthood and even of royalty."[2]

NAMES IN THE BIBLE

DURING BIBLICAL TIMES, people had only one name and every child was given a freshly minted name that was entirely his or her own. Over a thousand years, there is only one Abraham, one Sarah, one

Miriam, one Solomon. None of the twenty-one kings of Judah was named after David, the founder of the dynasty.

There are 2,800 personal names in the Bible, of which fewer than 5 percent are used today.[3] Biblical names are a wonderfully mixed bag. Many are theophoric—exalting God. Names with the prefixes or suffixes *el, eli, ya, yahu* all refer to the Holy One: Elisha—God is my salvation; Raphael—God has healed; Netanyahu—gift of God.

Some biblical names describe the particular circumstances of a child's birth. Moses means "because I drew him out of the water." Chava (Hebrew for Eve) comes from the root word for life, "because she was the mother of all living generations."

Names inspired by nature abound in the Bible: Deborah—bee; Jonah—dove; Tamar—palm tree. This tradition has been revived with a passion in modern Israel where the natural landscape has inspired many beautiful names: Tal and Tali—dew; Elon and Elana—oak; Oren—fir tree; Namir—leopard.

SACRED AND SECULAR

DESPITE THEIR IMPORTANCE and durability, biblical Hebrew names have always competed with names from other languages and cultures. Even during the Talmudic period (200 B.C.E. to 500 C.E.),* Aramaic, Greek and Roman names outnumbered biblical names among Jews. During the Middle Ages in Eastern Europe, Jewish males were usually given both a secular (*kinnui*) and a religious name (*shem ha-kadosh*). Eventually, the secular name became so dominant that some parents did not bother with Hebrew, a devel-

---

*C.E., which stands for Common Era, is a way of discussing the centuries without referring to the divinity of Jesus, as does A.D., "Anno Domini, the year of our Lord." B.C.E. means "before the common era."

opment that alarmed the rabbis so much that they decreed that every boy should be given a Hebrew name.[4]

It remained common, however, for men to have two names: one for use in the gentile world, the other for religious purposes. While Hebrew names were usually given to honor a family member (see below), the process for selecting secular names varied. The most straightforward method was to seek a direct translation of a Hebrew name; thus in France, men called Chaim* in synagogue were often known as Vive* on the street. In Germany, the use of the first name Wolf was probably based on the biblical Benjamin, whose tribe was associated with that animal. However, it was also common to select a secular name only because it sounded something like a Hebrew name, or shared a letter or two with a Hebrew name, or simply because it was popular in the surrounding culture.

Girls rarely had two names. The one that sufficed was often, though by no means always, Hebrew. And through constant use, some Yiddish names took on the venerable status of biblical ones. Feigel, for example, a very popular name among many of our Polish great-grandparents, has an obscure etymology and may be based on words meaning violet, bird or even fig.[5] These Yiddish names often pose a problem for modern parents who search for the Hebrew equivalent of Grandma Bayla's name when she never had one.

Customs differed in the Sephardic (Spanish and Mediterranean) world. Although the girls were commonly given only a non-Hebrew name, boys in Syria would never be called by an Arabic name only. Equivalents in Hebrew and Arabic would be hyphenated, as in Shelomo-Shelem (peace) or Yehuda-Aslan (lion).[6]

Throughout history, Hebrew names have remained essential to the prayer life of Jewish men, for being called to the Torah in the synagogue, and for use on legal documents such as *ketubot* (marriage

*"Life."

contracts). It was also essential to know the Hebrew names of both one's parents; in the memorial service for the dead, the name of the departed's father is invoked, and in the special prayer recited on behalf of the sick, the name of the patient's mother is included. Besides, since it was thought that the angels speak only Hebrew, one had to know his Hebrew name in order to gain access to heaven.

With emancipation in Europe, names were more readily taken from society at large, softening the lines between Jews and gentiles. By the end of the nineteenth century in Northern Europe, and in early twentieth century America, there developed a whole new category of Jewish-gentile names. Jews seemed drawn to certain names. In pre-World War I Germany, for example, Ludwig, Moritz, and Siegfried were so identified with Jews that non-Jews began to avoid them. Isadore (which actually means "gift of Isis") was a very popular *kinnui* for Isaac and Israel, and became so identified with the Jews that it became a Nazi epithet.[7] In America, Hymie, a nickname for Hyman, which was a popular Americanization of Chaim, became an anti-Semitic slur as well.*

Jewish immigrants to America often selected new names when they arrived in the *goldene medina*, the golden land. Although some traditional names (Abraham and Sarah, for example) never completely disappeared, many Yiddish and Hebrew names seemed too foreign, too "green" for the new country. So the Yiddish Blume (flower) blossomed into Rose, Lily, and Iris. The old country Tzvi (deer) who might have been known as Hersch (deer) in Yiddish, became Harry, Hyman, and Henry.

For the past few generations in America, Jews have tended to give

---

*The history of Jewish surnames is another fascinating story. It was not until the Middle Ages in Europe that Jews commonly added family names, mostly to facilitate dealings with the non-Jewish world. In Northern Europe, Jews did not use surnames until the nineteenth century, often under compulsion by Christian authorities.

children both a secular English name and a Hebrew name. Often, the two share nothing but the initial letter or sound. A baby girl named for her grandmother Shayna can be Sandra or Susan. A boy named for Uncle Moshe may be called to the Torah as Moshe, but his teachers and friends will know him as Mark. While many rabbis find this custom silly or even repugnant, "phonetic assimilation" actually has ancient precedents; under Greek rule, Menachem became Menelaus.

"THE MEMORY OF THE RIGHTEOUS IS A BLESSING"

ALTHOUGH THE CUSTOM of naming children after parents or grandparents is not found in the Bible, the practice dates all the way back to the Egyptian Jews of the sixth century B.C.E., who most likely borrowed the idea from their neighbors. Naming a child after a relative has been an almost universal Jewish practice ever since, though with a fundamental difference between Jews of Ashkenazic (Eastern European) descent, and Sephardic Jews.

Ashkenazic Jews name children only after dead relatives, and Sephardic Jews name them after the living. The difference is probably based in two very different attitudes toward the angel of death. Ashkenazic Jews avoided naming children after living relatives for fear that the grim reaper would take a child in place of a grandfather. But Sephardic Jews assumed the angel of death might actually err in favor of longevity for both generations if grandfathers and grandsons bore the same name.

In some Sephardic communities, naming children is done in a precise pattern; the first son is named after the father's father, the first daughter is named after the father's mother, the second son is named after the mother's father, the second daughter after the mother's mother. After that, names are selected to honor any family member or friend.[8]

Since the vast majority of American Jews are of Ashkenazic descent, however, the custom of naming after a deceased relative is most common in the United States. Many people give their babies the same Hebrew name as a beloved grandmother or grandfather, and then select a secular name on the basis of the initial letter or sound of the Hebrew. Which is how it comes to pass that Baruch ("blessed") becomes Barry, Bradley, Bruce, and even Brian, which is a Celtic or Gaelic name that means strength. And one Grandma Naomi of blessed memory was honored with a namesake called Natalie, which means Christmas Child.

The ancient practice of naming to honor someone has recently been included in Jewish baby announcements. For example:

> *Karen Appel and Mark Fine*
> *joyfully announce the birth of their daughter*
> *Abigail Appel Fine*
> *May 25, 1984   23 Iyar 5744*
> *Named after Mark's paternal grandfather Abraham Fine*

Another announcement simply included the line, "Ruth Doviva is named after Marty's grandmother Rivka and Myra's grandfather Dov."

SUPERSTITION

NAMES HAVE BEEN associated with witchcraft since the beginning of human speech, probably due to the global suspicion that the soul is identical with and identified by a person's name. In some cultures, a secret name—one that expresses a person's true self—is given at birth and guarded against enemies and evil forces.

Superstitions about the power of names abound in Jewish culture and are even acknowledged in the Talmud, which states, "Four things can abrogate the fate of man and they are charity, supplication, change of name, and change of action." Thus, it was thought that when the angel of death came looking for someone, a shrewd person would say, "I am not the person you are seeking. I am not the one who committed the sins you charge me with."

Given the high infant mortality rate of earlier times, it is easy to understand why death and demons were thought to be particularly drawn to babies. So names were often employed to fool the angel of death. In Poland, newborn boys who were ill or somehow at risk were given name like Alte and Alter (another, or old one) or Zaide (grampa) to confuse death and evil spirits like Lilith, who reputedly roamed the earth searching for Jewish infants to kill. Not only would such a name confuse death, who came looking for a baby but find an old man instead, it also implied that the child would fulfill the name and live many years. Similarly, a name like Chaim (life) was given as a talisman.

Modern American Jews, who mock such medieval fantasies, in practice tend to follow the advice of the medieval pietist Rabbi Judah HaHasid who wrote, "Although one should not believe in superstitions, it is better to be careful." Which explains the many couples who refuse to have a crib in the house before the baby is born lest they tempt the evil eye, and parents who would no sooner consider naming their baby after a living grandparent than leave a newborn outside in a snowstorm.

FASHION

THROUGHOUT HISTORY, rabbis and scholars have bemoaned the demise of "authentic" Jewish names and warned against the assimilationism of secular names. But the mishmash of Jewish naming is at least as old as the first century of the Common Era.

Throughout history, names have been as vulnerable to fashion as hemlines. The Talmudic period saw a burst of new Hebrew names (Meir, Nahman, Ahavah) as well as a revival of obscure ones (Hillel and Gamliel). But even then, many Jews were giving their babies distinctly non-Jewish names from the vernacular, which for many generations was Aramaic.

It would be simple-minded to view only the most ancient Hebrew names as kosher. Jewish names were not handed down from Sinai, they have been hammered out of history. Take, for example, that extremely Jewish name, Esther. Esther is Persian in origin and shares its root with Astarte and Ishtar, the great fertility goddess of the ancient Middle East. Although Esther is translated to Hadassah in Hebrew, no one could argue the Jewish pedigree of Esther. Mordechai, the other hero of the Purim story, has a Persian name—and an idolatrous one at that. Mordecai means "devotee of the god Marduk."

The Jewish use of non-Jewish names has been a constant source of irritation to those who consider themselves conservators of the tradition. The Hellenization of Jewish names (Jason for Joshua) dismayed the rabbis of late antiquity. Alexander, a name with no Jewish lineage, has enjoyed a loyal following since biblical times and continues to be extremely popular.

Every generation adopts a new set of names that reflect the changing fashion of the times. In America, the children of Rose, Molly, Sophie, Sam, Max, and Jacob were Sylvia, Rosalyn, Muriel, Arthur, Charles, and Leonard. They in turn named children Ellen, Gail, Karen, Alan, Barry, and Ken, who raised the generation of Kim, Jennifer, and Stacy, Bradley, Joshua, and Jesse. The appearance and increasing use of middle names among Jews in America reflects a national trend.

The most recent pattern of Jewish American naming is a return to roots. Biblical names such as Sarah, Benjamin, Rebecca, and Aaron are enjoying enormous popularity today. And there has also been a run on selected "ethnic" immigrant names that "feel" Jewish. A rash of baby announcements proclaims a new generation of Roses, Lilies, Maxes, and Sams. Another new fashion, especially among Jews who have spent time in Israel, is to give babies modern Hebrew names.

Today, rabbis of all denominations tend to advocate the selection of an identifiably Jewish name. One of their most compelling arguments is that names like Ruth, David, Shulamit, and Raphael simplify life because they work well in the three settings American Jews are likely to inhabit: in thoroughly American situations like public school; in religious life, as when one is called to the Torah; and as visitors to—or residents of—Israel.

MODERN HEBREW NAMES

WITH THE ESTABLISHMENT of the State of Israel came the reconstruction of Hebrew as a modern language and a major retooling of Jewish names. Many who came to Palestine after the Holocaust were anxious to cast off all reminders of the Diaspora—especially German names. Some people translated themselves from Yiddish to Hebrew: Shayna (pretty one) became Yaffa, Gittel (good one) became Tova. Others simply chose a Hebrew name, and reversing the old custom they picked on the basis of a sound or letter. So Mendel and Morritz became Menachem and Meir.

The first generation of sabras (people born in Israel) inspired a host of names. There were lots of translations—a baby girl named for her aunt Raizel (rose) would be called Varda. And there was a resurrection of ancient biblical names that had not been heard for generations; Amnon, Yoram, Avital, Tamar. Even names of evil biblical characters surfaced, such as Aviram, who was swallowed by the earth in retribution for his instigation of the rebellion against Moses.

As the people gave life to the land, the land gave names to their babies: Kinereth, (a sea), Arnon, (a wadi), Barak (lightning), and Ora (light). Girls' names were grafted from boys' names: Ariella from Ariel, Gabriella from Gabriel. And there are several that serve both boys and girls including: Yona—dove, Ayala and Ayal—deer, Leor and Leora—light, Liron and Lirona—song.

The self-consciousness that Jewish history was being made also led to the creation of names like Aliyah (wave of immigration), Or-Tzion (light of Zion), and even Balfour and Balfouria (for the British Foreign Secretary who issued a declaration announcing England's favorable attitude toward the establishment of a Jewish state in Palestine).

Israelis feel much freer to invent and modify names. A recent trend has been the addition of a final *tav* or "t" sound to the end of virtually all girls' names, adding an extra feminine emphasis. Another current fashion is extremely obscure biblical names—of people and places. There are Israeli children called Hagar—the name of Abraham's non-Jewish concubine, and the mother of Ishmael.

Even the most venerated biblical names are open to reinterpretation. One American who moved to Israel wrote, "It is of course the traditional names that give rise to all those icky diminutives: Yosef (Yossi), Avraham (Avi,) Yaakov (Kobi), Yitzchak (Itzik and Tzachi). David inevitably becomes . . . Dudu, which to me always evokes a disposable diaper.

"Rachel meanwhile yields Racheli and Rochi, Shoshana is truncated to Shoshi, Ruth Ruti, Channah Channi, and my own Esther becomes Esti."[9]

ADOPTION AND NAMING

INCREASING NUMBERS OF American Jews are building their families through adoption. Generally, there is no difference in the ways adoptive parents and birth parents select names. All the same superstitions, customs, and arguments apply, which explains why American Jews tend to name adoptive children in memory of family members who have died.

Typically, a child's full Hebrew name includes his or her adoptive parents' names as well, as in *David ben Moshe v' Rivka*, David the son of Moses and Ruth; or *Gila bat Raphael v' Leah*, or Gila, the daughter of Raphael and Leah.

Sometimes, however, the custom used for adult converts is followed: *David ben Avraham Aveinu v' Sara Amenu*, David the son of Abraham our father and Sarah our mother. This "generic" convert's name was more common in the past, when adopted children were likely to be born Jews. Since ritual statuses—like that of *kohane* and *levi*—are inherited biologically, the rabbis wanted to be certain there would be no confusion if a child took the last name of his adoptive Cohen or Levinson parents.

Adoption announcements sometimes follow the new custom of explaining for whom the new child is named. By including the name or names of those whose memory is being honored, you can help people understand how this graft on your family tree is no less integral to its life—and to the community of Israel—than a biological child.

For more information about Jews and adoption, contact the Stars of David, a national, nonprofit social support network for Jewish adoptive families. Founded in 1984, Stars of David grew from one family to five hundred families in three years. Chapters exist in many states, from Connecticut to California. For more information, write to Stars of David, c/o Temple Shalom Emeth, 16 Lexington Street, Burlington, MA 01803. (Stars of David is *not* an adoption agency.)

✿ The List and How to Use It

No COMPILATION of Jewish names can be complete. The list that follows is not a scholarly work or a definitive dictionary, but a guide and tool for parents seeking a name for a Jewish child of the English-speaking world of the late twentieth century. Not all of the 2,800 names that appear in the Bible are listed. For instance, you will not find the long suffering Job here. Nor can there be any comprehensive catalog of modern Hebrew names; Israeli society propagates new ones so quickly, any list is incomplete before the ink dries. The names below reflect the author's best effort to catalog names that conform to current tastes, trends, and fashions in America today.

While you may find all the help you need on the following pages, there are other places to turn. The best published resource is *The Complete Dictionary of English and Hebrew Names* by Alfred J. Kolatch (Jonathan David Publishers, 1984). A volume of nearly five hundred pages, Kolatch's book includes a remarkable Hebrew vocabulary index, so if you wish your baby's name to reflect a quality, like compassion, suggestions appear under that heading. Rabbis, cantors, and *mohels* can be wonderful resources. And if you want some advice in selecting a modern Hebrew name, talk to an Israeli.

All the names on the list that follows have a Jewish pedigree of some sort—though with a little effort, you can find a Jewish precedent for almost any name, including Christian. Legend has it that some Danish Jews named their sons Christian to honor the courage of King Christian X, who wore the yellow badge when the Nazis forced them on the Jews of Denmark.[10]

In addition to biblical names, you will find traditional and modern Hebrew names, some Yiddish and some Sephardic names. Also included are a handful of ethnic English-language names, which are associated with American *Yiddishkeit* and have experienced a renaissance in the last few years.

Many of the names that appear are beautiful in both sound and meaning: Eliora (God is my light), Gila (joy), Rimona (pomegranate). Then again, some are simply melodic. For example, Aderet, which sounds lovely, means cape. And Leah means weariness. Unlike Americans, however, Israelis do not rule out names just because they have an unhappy literal meaning or biblical source. Hence the renaissance of the ill-fated Dina and the little-known Naphtali.

For many generations, children born on Jewish holidays were given names appropriate to the dates of their birth. Thus, babies were named Shabbatai (Sabbath), Pesach (Passover), and Yom Tov (holiday). It was a safe bet that anyone called Mordecai or Esther arrived during Purim. Those names have fallen far out of fashion with a majority of American Jews, but since they still have currency in Israel, some of these appear below.

Fashion, by definition, changes if not with the seasons, at least with each generation. Names considered unthinkably old-fashioned only a decade ago have been reclaimed with a vengeance—just go count the Sarahs and Aarons in the synagogue nursery school.

Speaking of Sarah, sources for girls' names reflect Judaism's undeniably patriarchal tradition. There are fewer female prophets, warriors, and priests in the Bible after whom to name daughters. And the paucity of historical records about female Jewish scholars, leaders, and public figures prior to the twentieth century compounds the problem. However, there is *yichus* (hereditary status) attached to certain women's names which date from more recent history. Emma, now quite popular, recalls two modern role models: the political activist Emma Goldman and the poet Emma Lazarus.

Of course, the greatest source of inspiration in naming a child may come from your own family's saga. Thus, great-grandma Pearl, who put her children through college by working in a sweatshop where she was a union organizer, is no less lofty a namesake than Avital, wife of King David. The names Pearl, Penina, or Margalit all would honor Grandma Pearl's memory and serve your daughter well.

Finally, a baby's name can be the excuse for an intergenerational or inter-*machatunim* (in-law) feud. It can also be a means of knitting two families together. There is no reason why the baby can't have more than one Hebrew name. Sharon Esther Rivka can honor her maternal great-grandmother and both her paternal great-aunts. And think how impressive it will sound when she is called to the Torah with all those significant, powerful names.

When using the name list remember:

The first version of each name is given in the most common English form, followed by alternative English spellings, followed by a transliteration of the Hebrew pronunciation if it differs significantly from the English. Unless otherwise noted, the translation is from Hebrew.

All English versions of Hebrew names are transliterations, which means there is no exact or correct spelling. Dina, Deena, Dena, Dinah are all fine. Choose the spelling you prefer, or make up your own.

In most—though not all—Hebrew names, the accent falls on the second syllable. Thus, *Adam. Oren.* There are many exceptions, however, so if you are unsure ask someone who is more familiar with the language.

A number of names have variations that change the meaning somewhat. Most common are the suffixes -i, -li, and -iel. For example, Ron, which means joy or song, becomes Roni (my joy), Ronli (joy is mine), Roniel (joy of God).

There is no "J" sound in Hebrew. Wherever a "J" appears, the Hebrew sound is "Y." Thus, Jonina is Yonina. In most cases, and especially where there is no common English version, such names are listed under "Y." However, where an English version is possible (Jasmine or Yasmin) both are given under the listing for "J."

A Son!

AARON, ARON, AHARON אהרן
Teaching, singing, shining, or
mountain. The Aramaic root
word means "messenger." Aharon
was the older brother of Moses
and Miriam. He was the first Is-
raelite high priest and progenitor
of all priests. Rabbinic tradition
stresses his love of peace. He is
said to have died at the age of
123 on Mount Horeb.

ABBA אבא
Father. It's rather like naming
your son "Daddy," but Israeli
statesman Abba Eban wears it
well.

ABEL אבל
Breath. The son of Adam and
Eve, and the ill-fated brother of
Cain.

ABIR אביר
Strong.

ABNER, AVNER אבנר
Literally, father of light. It signifies brightness and light. Avner ben Ner was King Saul's
uncle, and the commander of his
army.

ABRAHAM, AVRAHAM אברהם
Father of a mighty nation. Abraham is known as the first Hebrew. The Hebrew letter Hay,
which appears twice in the unpronounceable name of God
(Yud Hay Vav Hay) was added
to his name, Abram, when he
accepted the covenant of Israel,
by circumcising himself and es-
tablishing the practice among his
people. The patriarch Abraham

is associated with *chesed*, loving-kindness, and with hospitality. The Arabic equivalent is Ali Baba. There are many nicknames associated with the name Abraham including Avi, Abe, Abie, and the Yiddish Avrom and Avrumke.

ABRAM, AVRAM   אברם
Abraham's original name.

ABSALOM, AVSHALOM אבשלום
Father of peace. King David's third son. A later Absalom played a prominent part in the defense of Jerusalem against the Emperor Pompey.

ACHIYA   אחיה
God is my brother. One of King David's warriors. The root/prefix, achi   or brother gives rise to a whole list of names not in common use.

ADAM   אדם
Earth. From its Phoenician and Babylonian origins, mankind. The first man. A name not popular among Jews until modern times.

ADIN   עדין
Beautiful, pleasant, gentle. A biblical name, it has a few variations, including Adi, Adina, Adino, Adiv.

ADLAI   עדלי
From the Aramaic, "refuge of God." The biblical Adlai was a shepherd.

ADMON   אדמון
The name of a red peony that grows in the upper Galilee.

AKIBA, AKIVA   עקיבה
Akiva is derived from the same root as Jacob, Ya'akov, which means supplanter, or "held by the heel." Rabbi Akiva was a first century scholar and teacher, the founder of a famous academy. Common nicknames include Koby and Kivi.

ALEXANDER   אלכסנדר
Protector of men. Ever since the third century B.C.E., when Alexander the Great spared Jerusalem from harm, Jewish boys have been named in his honor. As the story goes, the high priest of Jerusalem was so grateful for

Alexander's largess, he proclaimed that all Jewish males born in the city for a full year would bear the conqueror's name. Ever since, Alexander, in various languages and forms, has remained popular. Sander is the Yiddish equivalent. The Russian diminutive, Sasha, is currently enjoying popularity in America as a name for girls as well as boys. Other nicknames include Alex, and Sandy.

ALON אלון
Oak tree. A very popular name in Israel. One of the sons of Shimeon.

ALYAN עלין
Heights. One of the sons of Seir in the Bible.

AMAL עמל
Work. A member of the tribe of Asher.

AMATZ, AMAZIAH אמץ, אמציה
Strong, courageous.

AMI עמי
My people. A popular Israeli name on its own, this root is

found in many other names, a few of which follow.

AMICHAI עמיחי
My people are alive.

AMIEL עמיאל
God of my people.

AMIKAM אמיקם
Nation arisen.

AMIN אמין
Trustworthy.

AMIR אמיר
Mighty, strong.

AMIRAM אמירם
My people are lofty.

AMITAI אמיתי
Truth, faithful. Amitai was the father of Jonah.

AMNON אמנון
Faithful. Amnon was the oldest son of David. Amnon of Mainz, a legendary figure and martyr of the tenth century C.E., is said to have composed the hymn *U'netanneh Tokef*.

AMOS   עמוס
Burdened. A prophet who preached in the Northern Kingdom of Israel during the eighth century, B.C.E. Social morality was his central theme. A very popular Israeli name.

AMRAM   אמרם
A mighty nation. Amram was the father of Moses, Miriam, and Aaron. The *Mahzor de Rav Amram*, written during the ninth century C.E., is one of the oldest surviving prayer books; the Gaon, as he was called, established the order of the siddur used to this day.

ARIEL   אריאל
Lion of God. Also a poetic name for the city of Jerusalem. Ari and Arik are diminutives.

ARNON   ארנון
Roaring stream. In the Bible, the Arnon was a stream in the frontier of the Moab.

ARYEH   אריה
Lion. The name Aryeh appears in the Bible, once as an officer in the army of Pekach. Ari, now a popular name in its own right in Israel, is a diminutive of Aryeh.

ASA   אסא
Healer. A king of Judea.

ASHER   אשר
Blessed, fortunate. Asher was the son of Jacob and Zilpah, and the leader of one of the twelve tribes of Israel. Anshel is the Yiddish.

AVI   אבי
Father. A diminutive of Avraham, but also used as a name on its own, this is the prefix/root for a great many names, some of which follow.

AVICHAI   אביחי
My father lives.

AVIDAN   אבידן
Father of justice or God is just.

AVIEL   אביאל
God is my father.

AVIEZER   אביעזר
Father helper.

AVIGDOR   אביגדור
Father protector. Popular in Israel.

AVIMELECH   אבימלך
Father king.

AVINOAM   אבינעם
Father of delight.

AVISHAI   אבישי
In Aramaic, "gift of God." A
grandson of the biblical Jesse.

AVISHALOM   אבישלום
Father of peace.

AVIV   אביב
Spring.

AZI   עזי
Strong.

AZRIEL   עזריאל
God is my help.

B   ב

BARAK ברק
Lightning. A biblical soldier during the reign of Deborah.

BARAM ברעם
Son of the nation.

BARUCH ברוך
Blessed. Baruch was friend and secretary to the prophet Jeremiah. The Yiddish version, Bendit, is actually based on the name Benedict. The philosopher Baruch Spinoza (1632–1677) was known as Benedict de Spinoza.

BEN-AMI בן־עמי
Son of my people. The prefix *ben* is attached to a number of words and names.

BENJAMIN, BINYAMIN בנימין
Son of my right hand. Benjamin was the youngest, and much-loved of Jacob's sons, his second child with Rachel, who died giving birth to him. He was the only brother of eleven who did not participate in Joseph's sale into slavery and was honored by having the Holy Temple built on territory allotted to his tribe.

BEN-ZION בן־ציון
Son of Zion. Benzi is a popular nickname.

BERYL בעריל
A Yiddish diminutive for bear. Also Ber. The Hebrew equivalent is Dov.

BOAZ   בעז

Strength and swiftness. The
great-grandfather of King David,

Boaz was a wealthy, land-owning
Bethlehemite who married Ruth.
(Ruth 2:4)

C 𝓮𝓼𝓽 ב

CALEB, CALEV   כלב
Heart, also dog. One of the twelve spies sent by Moses to reconnoiter Canaan. Only he and Joshua brought back a favorable report, for which they were allowed to enter the promised land.

CHAIM, HAYYIM   חיים
Life.

D   ד

DAN   דן
Judge. Dan was the fifth son of Jacob, and first-born of Bilhah, Rachel's maidservant. Dani is a variant.

DANIEL   דניאל
God is my judge. The Book of Ezekiel mentions a pious and wise Daniel, who predated Moses. Daniel, the hero of the Book of Daniel, was known as an interpreter of visions.

DAVID   דוד
Beloved. David was the shepherd anointed by the prophet Samuel as the future king. His career began with the killing of Goliath; his popularity aroused King Saul's jealousy. King first of Judah and later of Israel, David created a loose national union of the tribes, eventually making Jerusalem his capital. One of the most beloved figures in Judaism, it is believed that the Messiah will be one of David's descendants. Since Talmudic times, his name has been a favorite.

DEROR, DERORI, DROR   דרור, דרורי
Freedom, Also, a bird. A popular Israeli name.

DEVIR   דביר
Holy place. In the Bible, Devir was a king of Eglon.

DOR   דור
A generation.

DORAN   דורן

Gift.

DOTAN   דותן

Law. In the Bible, Dotan was a

place in Palestine, north of Samaria.

Dov   דב

Bear. Dubi is a popular Israeli nickname. (See also Beryl)

E   א

EFRAYIM, EFRAIM, EPHREM, EPHRAIM אפרים
Fruitful. Efrayim was one of Jacob's grandsons. His name is mentioned in the traditional Friday night blessing over sons.

EFRON עפרון
A bird.

ELAZAR אלעזר
God has helped. Aaron's third son, Elazar became the high priest. There have been many famous Elazars throughout history, including Elazar ben Jair, a commander in Masada, whose eloquence persuaded the city's defenders that suicide was preferable to surrender or defeat.

ELI, ELY עלי
Ascend. In the Bible, Eli was a high priest and the last of the Judges in the days of Samuel.

ELIAKIM אליקים
God established.

ELIEZER אליעזר
My God has helped. The name Eliezer appears three times in the Bible: Abraham's steward, Moses' son, and a prophet in the time of Jehosaphat. The name belonged to three great Talmudic scholars and many great German rabbis.

ELIHU אליהוא
He is my God. The name Elihu appears several times in the

Bible, once as a young friend of Job.

ELIJAH, ELIAHU   אליהו

The Lord is my God. Elijah was a prophet who lived in the time of Ahab and Jezebel during the ninth century B.C.E. and led the fight against the cult of Baal. He ascended to heaven in a chariot of fire, but, according to tradition, did not die and continues to accompany Israel in her exile. He is often disguised as a poor beggar. Elijah's presence is invoked during Passover and at circumcisions. He is viewed as a herald of the Messiah.

The name has many translations: in German, it is Elias; in French, Elie; in Italian, Elia. In English, Eliot, Ellis, and Elias are all based on the name Elijah. Elya is a common Israeli nickname.

ELISHA   אלישע

God is my salvation. Elisha the prophet succeeded Elijah. In Second Kings, there are miraculous stories about his long life.

ELKANAH   אלקנה

God brought.

EMANUEL, EMMANUEL   עמנואל

God is with us.

ENOCH   חנוך

Dedicated. Enoch was Cain's son, born after Abel died.

ESHKOL   אשכול

A cluster of grapes. In Hebrew letters, Eshkol signifies a gathering of scholars. Levi Eshkol was Israeli prime minister from 1963 to 1969.

ETAN, EYTAN   איתן

Strong.

EVEN   אבן

Stone. Eben and Eban are variants.

EYAL   איל

A stag.

EZEKIEL   יחזקאל

God will strengthen. Ezekiel was a prophet who lived during the sixth century, B.C.E., toward the end of the first Temple. Ezekiel's description of the Divine Throne was the major text for Jewish mysticism *(Ma'aseh Merkavah)*.

EZRA, EZRI   עזרא, עזרי
Help. A priest and scribe of the fifth century B.C.E. who led a return from Babylon to Jerusalem, where he became a key figure in the reconstruction of the Temple and religious life. He has been compared in importance with Moses for his observance and instruction in Torah, and for having introduced the square Hebrew alphabet.

G ⟡ ג

GABRIEL, GAVRIEL גבריאל
God is my strength. Gabriel is
the angel that visited Daniel. In
Israel, the diminutive Gabi is
also used as a full name. Gavirol
is a Sephardic variation, Gavri is
a nickname.

GAD גד
Happy. Gad was one of Jacob's
sons. Also, Gadi, a diminutive.

GAL, GALI גל, גלי
A wave or a mountain. Also,
Galya.

GAMALIEL, GAMLIEL גמליאל
God is my reward. The name of
many Talmudic scholars.

GAN גן
Garden.

GARON גרון
A threshing floor. Guryon is a
variation.

GEDALIA, GEDALIAH, גדליה,
GEDALIAHU גדליהו
God is great. Gedaliah was a gov-
ernor of Judea.

GERSHOM, GERSON גרשום, גרשון
I was a stranger there. Moses
named his older son Gershom,
referring to the experience in
Egypt. The name has served
many teachers, including Gershom Scholem, the great twen-
tieth-century scholar of mystical
Judaism.

GIBOR גיבור
Strong, hero.

GIDEON גדעון
A mighty warrior. Gideon was a warrior-hero, reputed to have fathered seventy sons. Gidi is a popular nickname.

GIL, GILL, GILI, GILLI גיל, גילי
Joy. Gili means "my joy."

GILAD, GILEAD, GILADI גלעד, גלעדי
From a place name, a mountain range east of the Jordan River.

GUR, GURI, GURIEL גור, גורי, גוריאל
Respectively, young lion, my young lion, and God is my lion. Guryon is another variation.

H

HADAR הדר
Adornment. A biblical king of Edom.

HANAN חנן
Grace or gracious. A shortened form of Yochanan.

HAREL הראל
Mountain of God. A biblical place name.

HASKEL, HASKELL השכל
Yiddish form of Ezekiel.

HERSCH, HERSH הערש
In Yiddish, a deer. The diminutives and variations of Hersch are numerous: Herschel, Hesh, Heshel, Herzl, Hirsh, Hirsch.

(See Tzevi, the Hebrew equivalent.)

HILLEL הלל
Praised. Hillel became a popular name in honor of the memory of the great Palestinian scholar born in Babylon in 75 B.C.E. Hilly is a popular nickname.

HIRAM חירם
Noble born. Hiram was king of Tyre, c. 969–936 B.C.E. He helped to plan, build, and equip the Temple in Jerusalem.

HOD הוד
Splendor, vigor. Hod was a member of the tribe of Asher. Popular in Israel.

I ע

IRA עירא
Descendants.

ISAAC, ITZAK, YITZHAK יצחק
Laughter. Isaac, one of the three
patriarchs, was the son of Abraham and Sarah, born to them
very late in life. He was the first
Jew to be circumcised on the
eighth day of life. The story of
his binding, the *Akeda*, is one
of the most provocative and
powerful of all biblical stories.
The name has remained popular, serving, among others, Isaac
Luria, the Safed mystic who established the Lurianic Kabbalah.
There are many nicknames: Ike,
Issa, and Yitz among them.

ISAIAH, YISHAYAHU ישעיהו
God is salvation. Isaiah was
prophet in Jerusalem in the 700s,
B.C.E. Isa is a popular nickname.

ISRAEL, YISRAEL, YISROEL ישראל
Wrestler with God. The name
given to Jacob after he wrestled
with the angel which became a
synonym for the Jewish people.

ISSACHAR יששכר
There is a reward. Issachar was
the son of Jacob and Leah, a
leader of one of the twelve tribes
of Israel.

53

ITAI, ITTAI   אתי
Friendly. Itai was one of David's
warriors.

ITIEL   איתיאל
God is with me. Itiel was a member of the tribe of Benjamin.

ITTAMAR   איתמר
Island of palm. A name that
signifies gracefulness. One of
the sons of Aaron. Ismar is an
Ashkenazic transliteration of the
name.

J*

JACOB, YACOV, YA'ACOV יעקב
Held by the heel, supplanter. The third of the patriarchs, his name was changed to Israel after his wrestling match with an angel. There are many equivalents, nicknames and derivatives for Jacob, among them: James, Jack, Jake, and Yankele.

JARED, YARED ירד
To descend.

JEDEDIAH, YEDAIAH ידידיה
The name of two priestly ances-tral houses mentioned in the list in the book of Nehemiah.

JEREMIAH, JEREMY, YIR'MIAHU ירמידהו
God will uplift. Jeremiah began to prophesy around 625 B.C.E. His gloomy forecasts aroused resentment and he spent many years in jail.

JESSE, YISHAI ישי
Wealthy. Jesse was the father of David, the grandson of Boaz and Ruth.

*What commonly appears in English as "J" is pronounced "Y" in Hebrew; thus, Jacob is Yacov. Many names that appear anglicized as J-names are listed under Y. The names that appear here, however, are well-known in English.

JETHRO, YITRO   יתרו
Abundance, riches. Father of Zipporah, and Moses' father-in-law, Jethro was a Midianite priest.

JOEL, YOEL   יואל
God is willing. Joel is one of the twelve minor prophets who preached in Judea.

JONAH, YONAH   יונה
Dove. Jonah was the prophet who traveled inside a whale. A complex biblical character.

JONATHAN, YONATAN   יונתן
God has given. Jonathan was the son of Saul. His friendship with David sets the stage for one of the most moving biblical stories. Yoni is a popular Israeli nickname.

JORDAN, YARDEN   ירדן
Descend. Jori is a popular Israeli nickname.

JOSEPH, YOSEF   יוסף
God will increase. The son of Jacob and Rachel, almost 25 percent of Genesis is devoted to Joseph's story. A dreamer as well

as a shrewd politician, his name has been a favorite throughout Jewish history. Jose, the Aramaic form of the name, was popular in Talmudic times.

JOSHUA, YEHOSHUA   יהשוע
The Lord is my salvation. Joshua succeeded Moses as the leader of the Hebrews to the land of Israel. Moses changed his successor's name from Hoshua by adding a *yud*, one of the letters of God's name; thus, Yehoshua.

JOSIAH, YOSHIAHU   יאשיהו
God has protected. Son of Amnon, Josiah became a king of Judah at the age of eight.

JUDAH, YEHUDA   יהודה
Praise. Judah was the fourth son of Jacob and Leah. In the Joseph story, he plays a special role, with Reuben and Benjamin, as a spokesman for his brother. Judah received special blessings from his father, Jacob. Yehuda is the source of the words Judaism, Jewish, and Jew. There have been many famous Judahs, including Judah Halevi, the Hebrew poet.

K ק

KADMIEL   קדמיאל
God is the ancient One.

KALIL   כליל
Crown or wreath.

KANIEL   קניאל
A reed or stalk. In Aramaic, Kaniel means spear. The name connotes strength.

KATRIEL   כתריאל
Crown of the Lord.

KENAN   קינן
To acquire. A nephew of Abraham in the Bible.

KOBY   קובי
A nickname for Jacob.

KOHAV   כוכב
Star.

KORE, KORIE   קורא
Quail, or to call.

L   ל

LABAN   לבן
White. Laban was Rebecca's brother, the father of matriarchs Rachel and Leah, grandfather of the twelve tribes of Israel. Also, an unsavory character.

LAVI   לביא
Lion.

LAZAR, LEYZER   לאזאר
A Greek form of Eliezer and a popular Yiddish name.

LEOR   לאור
I have light.

LEV   לב
Heart in Hebrew. Lion in Yiddish, where Label is a nickname.

LEVI   לבי
Attendant. The name Levi signifies devotion. In the Bible, he was the third of Jacob's sons born to Leah. His descendants became the Levites, the priests, in the Temple.

LIRON   לירון
Song is mine.

LOTAN   לוטן
To envelop, or protect. Popular in Israel.

M

MAIMON מימון
Aramaic for luck or good fortune. The philosopher Moses ben Maimon, known as Maimonides, is the most illustrious bearer of the name.

MALACHI מלאכי
Messenger or angel. The last of the prophets.

MALKAM מלכם
God is their King.

MATTATHIAS, MATTITYAHU מתתיהו
Gift from God. A name linked to Chanukah, Mattathias was the father of Judah Maccabee and the patriarch of the Hasmonean dynasty. Common nicknames include Matt, Matti, Matia.

MAX
Once a common name among Jewish immigrants in America, Max has recently regained its popularity here. It is not a Hebrew name but is often given in association with the Hebrew Moshe.

MEGED מגד
Goodness, sweetness.

MEIR, MEYER מאיר
One who shines.

MENACHEM מנחם
Comforter. A biblical king known for his cruelty, Menachem was the name given to boys born on the 9th of Av, the day of mourning for the destruction of the

Temple. Yiddish derivatives include Mendel and Mannes.

MENASSEH, MANASSEH, MENASHE   מנשה
Causing to forget. The older of Joseph's sons, Menasseh and his brother Ephraim are mentioned in the Sabbath blessing over sons.

MERON   מרון
Troops. Also a town in Israel; popular name there today.

MICAH   מיכה
Who is like God. Micah was a prophet in Judah during the eighth century B.C.E., who denounced oppression by the ruling classes.

MICHAEL   מיכאל
Who is like God. Michael was the angel closest to God, and God's messenger who carried out divine judgments. Variationson Michael include Mike, Mickey, Mitchell, and the Russian, Misha.

MIRON   מירן
A holy place.

MORDECHAI   מרדכי
Persian for warrior or warlike. Mordechai was Queen Esther's cousin, who advised her on the saving of the Jews. It was a name commonly given boys born during Purim. Yiddish nicknames include Mottel, Motke, and Mordke. Motti is the Israeli pet name.

MORI   מורי
My teacher. Also a variation on Morrey, a nickname for Maurice or Morris, which is an anglicization of Moses.

MOSES, MOSHE   משה
Saved from the water. Or Egyptian for son or child. The leader and teacher who brought the Israelites out of bondage in Egypt. Variations on the name include Moss, Mose, Moise (French), and Moishe (Yiddish). Jewish immigrants to America named their Moishes Milton, Melvin, Morris, Maurice.

N נ

NAAMAN   נעמן
Sweet, beautiful. A general in the army of Aram.

NACHMAN   נחמן
Comforter.

NACHUM, NAHUM   נחום
Comforted. A prophet in the seventh century, B.C.E. Little is known about him.

NADAV   נדב
Benefactor.

NAMIR   נמיר
Leopard.

NAOR   נאור
Light.

NAPHTALI, NAFTALI   נפתלי
To wrestle. Jacob's sixth son by Bilhah.

NATHAN   נתן
He gave. Nathan was one of the minor prophets, who, together with Zadok the priest, anointed Solomon king. In Yiddish, the name is Nusan.

NATHANIEL   נתנאל
Gift of God. Nathaniel was the fourth son of Jesse and David's brother.

NAVON   נבון
Wise.

NEHEMIAH, NECHEMYA   נחמיה
Comforted of the Lord. Nehemiah served as a governor of

Judea, and was involved in rebuilding the walls of Jerusalem.

NIMROD   נמרוד
Hunter.

NIR, NIREL, NIRIA, NIRIEL
ניר, ניראל, ניריאל
Plow or plowed field. Niriel means the tilled field of the Lord.

NISSAN   ניסן
Flight, also emblem. Nissan is also the name of the lunar month in which Passover falls. Nisi is a popular nickname.

NISSIM   נסים
Miracles. A popular Sephardic name in Israel.

NITZAN   ניצן
Bud.

NIV   ניב
Aramaic and Arabic for speech.

NOAH   נח
Rest, quiet, or peace. As the only righteous man of his time, Noah and his family survived the great flood sent by God to punish an evil world. Noah was the first to plant a vineyard. It is pronounced Noach in Hebrew.

NOAM   נועם
Sweetness, friendship.

NUR, NURI   נור, נורי
Of Aramaic origin, fire. Also Nuria, Nurieh, and Nuriel, which means fire of the Lord.

O / ע

OBADIAH, OVADIAH, OVED
עובדיה, עובד
Servant of God. Obadiah was one of the twelve minor prophets and the author of the Bible's shortest book.

OFER עפר
A young deer.

OMRI עמרי
From the Arabic for "to live long." Omri was a king in Israel during the 800s B.C.E.

OREN, ORIN, ORRIN, ORON ארן
Fir tree, cedar. A popular Israeli name.

OZ, OZNI עוז, אזני
Strength, hearing. Ozni was a son of Gad, a grandson of Jacob.

P

PALTI, PALTIEL, PILTAI

פלטי, פלטיאל, פלטי

My deliverance. A common name in the Bible. Palti was Michal's second husband, Piltai a member of a priestly family.

PERETZ פרץ
Burst forth.

PESACH פסח
Pass over. A name often given boys born during the holiday of Pesach.

PINCHAS, PINCUS פנחס
Dark-complexioned. Pinchas (Phineas in Greek) was a priest, a grandson of Aaron.

R   ר

RAANAN   רענן
Fresh, luxuriant.

RACHIM, RACHAMIM   ,רחים
רחמים
Compassion. A common name among Sephardic Jews.

RAMIE   רימי
Abbreviation of Avram.

RANEN, RANON   רנן, רנון
To sing.

RAPHAEL   רפאל
God has healed. Raphael is one of the four archangels. According to the Talmud, he was one of the three angels who visited Abraham, and he is associated with healing. Also spelled Rafael and Refael; Rafi is a popular nickname.

RAVID   רביד
Ornament.

RAVIV   רביב
Rain or dew.

RAZ, RAZI, RAZIEL   רז, רזי, רזיאל
From the Aramaic for secret.

REUBEN, REUVEN   ראובן
Behold, a son. Jacob and Leah's first son.

RIMON   רימון
Pomegranate.

RON, RONEL, RONI, RONLI
רון, רונאל, רוני, רונלי
Song and joy, in various settings.

S 𓂂 ס

SAADAH, SAADYA   סעדיה
Aramaic for Ezra, meaning
God's help. Saadiah ben Joseph was a great Egyptian-born
scholar of the ninth century. A
popular Sephardic name.

SAGI   שגיא
Sublime.

SAMSON, SHIMSHON   שמשון
Sun, signifying strength. Strong-
man Samson, most famous for
his betrayal by Delilah, was from
the tribe of Dan.

SAMUEL, SH'MUEL   שמואל
God has heard. Samuel was the
son of Hannah, raised by the
priest Eli. A prophet and judge,

he anointed King Saul and later
King David. Samuel was the last
of the Judges.

SAUL, SHA'UL   שאול
Borrowed. Saul was the first king
of Israel, from the tribe of Benjamin.

SETH, SHET   שת
Appointed. The name comes
from the line "Because God appointed me another seed beside
Abel." Seth was Adam's son,
born after Abel's death.

SHAI   שי
Gift.

SHALOM, SHOLOMO, SHOLOM, SHLOMI שלום, שלמה, שלומי
Peace.

SHAMIR שמיר
Strong.

SHRAGA שרגא
Light, in Aramaic.

SIMCHA שמחה
Joy. Also a girl's name.

SIMON, SIMEON, SHIMON, SHIMEON שמעון
To hear or be heard. Shimon was the second son born to Jacob and Leah. (Simon is the Greek version.) Simi is a popular nickname for Shimon in Israel.

SIVAN סיון
The seventh month, whose symbol in the horoscope is Gemini.

SOLOMON שלמה
Peace. Solomon, the son of David and Bathsheba, is the poet who wrote Song of Songs, Proverbs, and Ecclesiastes. His reputation for wisdom—especially in resolving the case where two women claimed the same child as their own—is enshrined in the adjective "solomonic."

T ט

TABBAI   טבאי
From the Aramaic word, good.
Names like Tov, Tovi, and Tavi
share the root and the meaning.

TAL, TALOR   טל, טל-אור
Dew, dew of light.

TAMIR   תמיר
Tall, like the tamar or palm tree.

TIMUR   תמור
Tall, also derived from the word
for palm tree.

TIVON   טבעון
Student of nature.

TOBIAH, TUV'YA   טוביה
The Lord is my God. Toby is the
popular nickname.

TZEVI   צבי
Deer. Also spelled Tzvi, Zvi,
and Zevi. Very popular in Israel.

U ✿ א

URI, URIEL אורי, אוריאל
From the root word light. According to *Midrash Rabbah,* Uriel is one of the four angels who reside around God's throne.

W ✒ ד

WOLF, WOLFE   וואלף   include Vulf and Velvel. (See
Yiddish for wolf, where variants   Ze'ev.)

Y 𝒆𝒔𝒕𝒚 י

YAKIR   יקיר
Beloved, honorable.

YALON   ילון
He will rest. A son of Caleb.

YAMIR   ימיר
To change.

YANIR   יניר
He will plow.

YARON   ירון
To sing.

YAVNIEL   יבניאל
God will build.

YEFET   יפת
Beautiful. Also spelled Yafet, Yaphet. Yefet was one of Noah's sons.

YEHIEL   יחיאל
May God live. Yehiel was chief musician in the court of King David.

YIFTACH   יפתח
Open.

YIGAL   יגאל
He will redeem. Popular in Israel.

YOAV   יואב
God is father. King David's nephew and an officer in his army.

YOCHANAN   יוחנן
God is gracious. There are more than fifty Yochanans mentioned in the Talmud.

YORAM   יורם
God is exalted.

YORAN   יורן
To sing.

YOTAM   יותם
A biblical name. One of Gideon's sons.

Z

ZACH   זך
Pure or clean.

ZACHARY, ZACHARIAH   זכריה
Remembering the Lord. The name of one of the minor prophets, and of a king of Judah and a king of Israel. Nicknames include Zack and Zeke.

ZALMAN   צלמון, זלמון
Yiddish for Shlomo.

ZAMIR   זמיר
Song, also nightingale.

ZAVDI, ZAVDIEL   זבדי, זבדיאל
My gift, gift of God. An officer in David's army.

ZEBULON, ZEVULON   זבולון
To exalt or honor. Zevulon was the sixth son of Jacob and Leah.

ZEDEKIAH   צדקיה
God is righteousness. A king of Judah.

ZE'EV, ZEV, ZEVI, ZEVIEL
   זאב, זאבי זאביאל
Wolf in Hebrew. (See Wolf.) Very popular in Israel.

ZEPHANIAH   צפניה
God has treasured. A seventh century prophet, Zephaniah belonged to the tribe of Judah.

ZERACH   זרח
Light rising.

73

ZION, TZION   ציון
Excellent, a sign. The name of
the whole Jewish people, and of
a mountain in Jerusalem.

ZIV, ZIVI   זיו, זיוי
To shine.

ZOHAR   זהר
Light, brilliance.

ZUSHYE, ZUSYA   זושע, זוסע
Yiddish for sweet.

A Daughter!

A

ABIGAIL, AVIGAIL אביגיל
Father's joy. Abigail was an early supporter of King David, even before she became his wife. She was known for her beauty, wisdom, and powers of prophecy.

ABIRA אבירה
Strong.

ABRA אברה
From the Hebrew root Abba or father. A diminutive of Abraham.

ADA, ADI עדה, עדי
Ornament.

ADENA, ADINA עדינה
Noble or adorned, gentle.

ADERET אדרת
A cape or outer garment.

ADIRA אדירה
Strong or mighty.

ADIVA אדיבה
Gracious, pleasant.

ADRA אדרה
From the Aramaic, glory or majesty.

ADVA אדוה
An Aramaic name that means wave or ripple.

AHARONA אהרנה
Feminine version of Aaron, which means teaching or singing. Variations include, Arona, Arni, Arnina, Arnit, Arninit.

77

AHAVA   אהבה
Love, beloved.

ALEEZA, ALIZA, ALITZA
עליזה, עליצה
Joy or joyous one.

ALEXANDRA   אלכסנדרה
Feminine of the Greek ruler
Alexander. See "Alexander" for
a full explanation of the name.
Queen Salome Alexandra was a
ruler of Judea from 76-67
B.C.E.

ALIYA, ALIYAH   עליה
To go up. When one is called
up to the Torah in the synagogue, one is given an aliyah.
Also, moving to Israel is called
making aliyah. The name Aliya
has been given to daughters by
refusenik parents in the Soviet
Union.

ALMA   עלמה
Maiden. In Spanish, it means
soul.

ALONA   אלונה
Oak tree. Alon is a popular boy's
name as well.

ALUMA, ALUMIT עלומה, עלומית
Girl or maiden.

AMALIA   עמליה
The work of the Lord.

AMIRA   אמירה
Speech. Ear of corn.

ANNA, ANN   חנה
These and many more (Annette,
Annie, Anita, Anya) are all
forms of the biblical name
Hanna. Anna is the Hellenized
version that spawned so many
derivatives.

ARELLA   אראלה
Angel, messenger.

ARIELLA   אריאלה
Lioness of God.

ARMONA, ARMONIT   ארמנה,
ארמנית
Castle or palace.

ARNA, ARNIT   ארנה, ארנית
Cedar.

ARNONA, ARNONIT   ארנונה,
ארנונית
From arnon, a roaring stream.

ARZA, ARZIT   ארזה, ארזית
Cedar beams.

ASHIRA   עשירה
Wealthy.

ATARA, ATARET   עטרה, עטרת
Crown.

ATIRA   עתירה
Prayer.

AVIELA, AVIELLA   אביאלה
God is my father.

AVITAL   אביטל
Dew of my father. One of King
David's wives.

AVIVA   אביבה
Spring. A popular Israeli name.
Avivit and Avivi mean spring-
like. Avivit is also the word for
lilac.

AVODA   עבודה
Work.

AYALA   אילה
Deer or gazelle.

AZA, AZAH, AZIZA   עזה, עזיזה
Strong.

B   ב

BAILA, BAYLE   ביילא
Yiddish form of Bilhah, one of
the four women who gave birth
to the tribes of Israel. The Latin
root means beautiful. Bella and
Belle are derivatives.

BAT-AMI   בת־עמי
Daughter of my people.

BATSHEVA   בת־שבע
Daughter of the oath. Batsheva
was one of David's wives, known
for her beauty. Solomon was
their second son. Batshuva is a
variant spelling and Basha is a
diminutive.

BATYA   בתיה
Daughter of God.

BENYAMINA   בנימינה
The feminine form of Benjamin.

BERIT, BE'RIT   בארית
Well.

BERURIAH, BERURYAH   ברוריה
Pure or clean. Beruriah lived in
the second century C.E. and was
renowned for moral stature and
intellectual incisiveness. She is
the only woman in Talmudic literature whose views were taken
seriously by her contemporaries.

BINA, BUNA   בינה, בונה
Understanding, intelligence.

BIRA   בירה
Capital.

BLUMA, BLUME בלומא
Yiddish, flower.

BRACHA ברכה
Blessing.

BONA בונה
Builder.

BRINA ברײנא
With joy. Based on the Slavic
Bronia.

C ב

CARMEL, CARMELLE, CARMELA, CARMELIT
כרמל, כרמלה, כרמלית
Vineyard. A very popular Israeli name with many variations: Carma, Carmit, Carmia.

CARNA, CARNIT קרנא, קרנית
Horn. Carniella means horn of God.

CHAVA הוה
Eve. Mother of life.

CHAYA חיה
Life.

CLARA כלרה
Yiddish, meaning clean.

D

DAFNA דפנה
Laurel.

DALIA, DALIT דליה, דלית
Branch.

DANIELLA, DANIELLE דניאלה
God is my judge. The feminine
version of Daniel has many derivatives: Dania, Dani, Danya,
Danit.

DANNA דנה
Judge. Feminine of Dan.

DANYA דניה
Feminine of Dan.

DAVIDA, DAVITA דוידה
The feminine of David, meaning
beloved or friend. Nickname,
Davi.

**DEBORAH, DEBRA, DEVORAH,
DEVRA** דבורה
To speak kind words or a swarm
of bees. Devorah was a prophetess and judge who led a revolt
against a Canaanite king. Her
composition, the "Song of Deborah," is one of the oldest known
Hebrew poems.

DEENA, DENA, DINA, DINAH
דינה
Judgment. Deena was the
daughter of Jacob and Leah, Jacob's only female offspring.

DEGANIA דגניה
Corn. Also the first kibbutz.

DELILA דלילה
Poor or hair. Delila was a Phil-
istine woman, Samson's mistress.

DERORA, DRORA   דרורה
Freedom.

DIZA, DITZA   דיזה, דיצה
Joy.

DODI, DODIE   דודי
Beloved, friend.

DORIT   דורית
Of this era. Very popular in Israel.

DORON, DORONIT   דורונית
Aramaic for gift.

DORYA   דוריה
Generation of God.

DOVA, DOVEVA, DOVIT
דובה, דובבה, דובית
Bear.

EDNA עדנה
Delight, pleasure. Edna appears in the book of Tobit, in the Apocrypha.

EFRAT אפרת
Honored, distinguished. The wife of Caleb.

EFRONA עפרונה
A songbird.

ELANA אילנה
Oak tree. Ilana is a variant English spelling.

ELIANA אליענה
God has answered me.

ELINOAR אלינער
God of my youth.

ELIORA אליאורה
God is my light.

ELISHEVA אלישבע
God is my oath. Elisheva was Aaron's wife, the matriarch of the priestly caste. The Hellenized form is Elizabeth, which has many nicknames and derivatives: Ella, Elisa, Eliza, Elise, Elsie, Betsy, Liz, Libby, Betty, Elyssa.

Elisheva Bikhowsky (1888–1949) was a Russian-born poet who settled in Israel in 1925, where she published in Hebrew.

EMANUELLA עמנואלה
God is with us.

EMMA   עמה
Originally from the Teutonic for grandmother or big one, the name was popular among Jewish immigrants to America at the turn of the century including the Russian-born anarchist writer and organizer Emma Goldman, and the poet Emma Lazarus. The name Emma is again popular in America but is not used in Israel.

EMUNA   אמונה
Faith.

ESTHER, ESTER   אסתר
From the Persian for star. Esther is the heroine of the story of Purim. She, with help from her cousin Mordechai, averted the annihilation of the Jews in her community. The Hebrew name for Esther is Hadassah, which means myrtle. Variations include Esta, Essie, Estelle, and Estella. Etti is a popular Israeli nickname.

EVA, EVE, CHAVA   חוה
Life. According to Genesis, Eve was the first woman, the mother of all human life.

EZRAELA   עזראלה
God is my help. The feminine for Ezra.

F **פ**

Frieda, Frayde, Freydel
Yiddish for joy.

פריידע, פריידעל

G ג

GABRIELLA, GAVRIELLA
גבריאלה
God is my strength. The feminine version of Gabriel, nicknames include Gabi and Gavi.

GALI, GALIT גלי, גלית
Fountain or spring.

GALYA גליה
God has redeemed.

GAMLIELA, GAMLIELLE גמליאלה
Feminine forms of Gamliel.

GANIT גנית
Garden.

GARNIT גרנית
Granary.

GAVRILLA גברילה
Heroine, strong.

GAYORA גיאורה
Valley of light.

GAZIT גזית
Hewn stone.

GEULA גאולה
Redemption.

GILA, GEELA גילה
Joy. Gilana and Gilat also mean joy. Gilia, a variant, means my joy is in the Lord.

GILADA גלעדה
My joy is forever.

GILI גילי
My joy.

GINA, GINAT גנה, גינת
Garden.

GITA, GITTEL   גיטע, גיטל
Yiddish, good one. (See Tova.)

GOLDA, GOLDE   גולדה
Yiddish for golden. The Hebrew
is Zahava.

GIVA, GIVONA   גבעה, גבעונה
Hill.

GURIT   גורית
Cub.

H* ‏ה

HADARA, HADURA
‏הדרה, הדורה
Splendid.

HADASS, HADASSAH ‏הדס, הדסה
Myrtle tree, which is a symbol of
victory. Esther's Hebrew name.
Nicknames include Dass and
Dasi.

HAGAR ‏הגר
Sarah's handmaid. Recently
popular in Israel.

HAGIT ‏חגית
Festive, joyous.

HAMUDA ‏חמודה
Precious.

HANNAH ‏חנה
Gracious, merciful. Hannah was
the mother of Samuel, wife of
Elkanah. Despairing because she
was barren, Hannah prayed at
the temple of Shiloh, where she
pledged that if granted a son she
would dedicate him to God's service. She gave birth to Samuel,
which means "God listened."
The Christian Bible refers to
Hannah as Anna. Thus, all the
variations of Ann, Anne, Annie,
Annette, Anita, are rooted in the
name, Hannah. Hanina.

*Nearly all these names begin with the sound "ch."

HASIA חסיה
Protected of the Lord.

HASIDA חסידה
Pious one. Also, stork.

HAVIVA חביבה
Beloved.

HEDVA חדוה
Joy.

HEDYA הדיה
Voice of the Lord.

HEFZIBA, CHEFTZEEBA חפצי־בה
My desire. The Hebrew pronunciation is pretty: Cheftzeeba.

HEMDA חמדה
Precious.

HERZLIA הרצליה
Yiddish for deer. The feminine version of a masculine name, it is also the name of an Israeli city. The name recalls Zionist leader Theodor Herzl.

HILA, HILLA הלה
Praise. Hillela is the feminine version of Hillel, which also means praise.

HILIT הילית
Glory or radiance.

HINDA הינדע
Yiddish for deer.

ן   ע

IDIT עדית
Choicest.

ILANA, ILANIT אילנה, אילנית
Oak tree. Elana is a variant English spelling.

IRIT עירית
Daffodil. Popular in Israel.

ISAACA יצחקה
Laughter. The feminine of Isaac.

ISRAELA, ISA ישראלה, ישה
The name of the people, almost always used in the diminutive, Isa.

ITI, ITTI אתי
With me.

J

JACOBA, YACOVA יעקבה
To supplant. The feminine of Yacov.

JASMINE, YASMIN יסמין
Persian flower name.

JEMINA, YEMINA ימינה
Right handed.

JESSIE, JESSICA, YISKA יסכה
God's grace.

JOHANNA, YOCHANA יוחנה
God is glorious. Feminine of Jochanan.

JONINA, YONINA יונינה
A dove.

JOSEPHA, YOSEFA יוספה
God will increase. The feminine of Joseph.

JUDITH, YEHUDIT יהודית
Praise. In an Apocryphal story, Judith was the heroine who saved Jerusalem by pretending to defect to the camp of General Holofernes, where she beheaded him while he slept.

K ב

KADIA, KADYA   כדיה
Pitcher.

KALANIT   כלנית
An Israeli plant with colorful flowers; anemone.

KANARIT, KANIT   כנרית, כנית
Songbird.

KARNA, KARNIT   קרנא, קרנית
Horn, as in ram's horn. A related name very popular in Israel is Keren.

KAYLA   קיילע
Yiddish form of Kelila. (See below.)

KELILA   כלילה
A crown of laurel, symbolizing victory.

KETZIA   קציעה
Fragrant. One of Job's daughters.

KINNERET   כנרת
Hebrew name of the Sea of Galilee. Also, harp.

KIRYA   קריה
Village.

KOHAVAH   כוכבה
Star.

L   ל

LAILA, LEILA, LILA   לילה
Night.

LEAH, LEA   לאה
In Hebrew it means weariness but in Assyrian it means mistress or ruler. The daughter of Laban, and Jacob's first wife, Leah is one of the four matriarchs of Judaism. She gave birth to six sons: Reuben, Simeon, Levi, Judah, Issachar, Zebulun, and one daughter, Dinah. Her marriage was the result of her father's trickery, substituting her for her sister, Rachel.

LEEBA, LIBA   ליבא
Yiddish for beloved. In Israel, the name also refers to the Hebrew root lev, which means heart.

LEORA, LIORA   ליאורה
Light, my light.

LEVANA, LIVANA   לבנה
Moon, or white. Popular among Sephardic Israelis.

LEVONA   לבונה
Spice or incense.

LIAN   ליאן
My joy.

LIAT   ליאת
You are mine.

LILY   לילי
Not a Hebrew name, popular name among American Jewish immigrants in the early twentieth century.

95

LIMOR   לימור
My myrrh.

LIRAZ   לירז
My secret.

LIVIA, LIVYA   לויה
A crown. When the accent falls
on the last syllable, Livia means
lioness. Also spelled Levia.

LIVNA   לבנה
From the word for "white."

LIVNAT   לבנת
From "white."

M

MAGDA   מגדא
A high tower.

MAHIRA, MEHIRA   מהירה
Energetic.

MALKAH   מלכה
Queen. A popular Sephardic name. (See Regina.)

MARGALIT   מרגלית
Pearl. (See Peninah.)

MARNI, MARNINA מרני, מרנינה
Rejoice.

MARVA   מרוה
Plant in the mint family.

MAYA   מיה
Water.

MAYTAL   מיטל
Waters of dew.

MAXIMA   מקסימה
Enchanter.

MERI   מרי
Rebellious.

MICHAELA   מיכאלה
Who is like God. Feminine of Michael, the name of one of the archangels. Mia is a nickname.

MICHAL   מיכל
A contraction of Michaela. Michal was the youngest daughter of King Saul, and wife of King David. At one point, Michal saved David from Saul's wrath.

97

MILI   מילי
Who is for me?

MIRA   מירה
Light. Feminine of Meir. Meira
and Meera are variations.

MIRIAM, MIRYAM   מרים
Sorrow or bitterness in Hebrew.
In Chaldean, mistress of the sea.
Miriam was a prophetess, singer,
and dancer, the sister of Moses

and Aaron. Nicknames include:
Mim, Mindy, Minna, Mira,
Mirel, Miri, Mirit, and Mollie.

MIRIT   מירית
Sweet wine.

MOR   מור
Myrrh.

MORIAH, MORIT מוריה, מורית
Teacher.

N

NAAMAH, NAAMIT נעמה, נעמית
Pleasant, beautiful.

NAAVA נאוה
Beautiful.

NADYA נדיה
From dowry. Used in Israel.

NAOMI נעמי
Beautiful, pleasant. In the Book of Ruth, Naomi was Elimelech's wife and the mother-in-law of Ruth. Naomi encouraged Ruth to marry her kinsman, Boaz.

NASIA, NASYA נסיה
Miracle of God.

NATANIA נתניה
Gift of God, feminine of Nathan.

NEDIVA נדיבה
Noble, generous.

NEHAMA נחמה
Comfort.

NEIMA נעימה
Pleasant.

NESYA נסיה
Yiddish for Nissan, the month of flowers.

NETA, NETIA נטע, נטיעה
A plant.

NETANYA נתניה
Gift of God.

NILI נילי
A plant.

99

NINA   נינה
In Hebrew, the word for grand-
daughter.

NIRA   נירה
Light.

NIRIT   נירית
A flowering plant.

NITZA   נצה
Bud.

NOA   נועה
Tremble, shake. A biblical name
popular in Israel today.

NOGA   נגה
Morning light.

NURIT   נורית
Buttercup.

O  א

ODELIA אודליה
I will praise God.

ORA, ORAH אורה
Light.

ODERA עודרה
Plow.

ORLI, ORLIT אורלי, אורלית
My light.

OPHIRA אופירה
Gold.

ORNA ארנה
Cedar.

OPHRAH, OFRA עפרה
Young deer.

P פ

PAZIT   פזית
Gold.

PENINAH, PENINIT פנינית **,**פנינה
Pearl or coral. Elkanah's second
wife. (See Margalit.)

PUAH   פועה
A midwife during the Egyptian
captivity, Puah and her colleague Shifra disobeyed Pharaoh's order to kill all male
Hebrews at birth.

R  ר

RACHEL   רחל
A ewe, symbol of gentility and purity. Rachel was the best-loved wife of Jacob, who gave birth to Joseph and Benjamin. She is described as "shapely and beautiful" but suffered barrenness for many years. The traditional site of her tomb near Bethlehem was venerated from at least the fourth century C.E. There have been many renowned Rachels, among them Rabbi Akiva's wife, a wealthy woman who, against her father's wishes, married the poor and at the time unlearned Akiva, and encouraged his study.

RAISA, RAIZEL   רייזא, רייזעל
Yiddish for Rose.

RAKEFET   רקפת
Cyclamen, a beautiful common flower in Israel.

RANANA   רעננה
Fresh.

RANIT, RANITA   רנית, רניתה
Joy or song.

RAPHAELA   רפאלה
God has healed. Feminine of Raphael.

RAYNA, REYNA   ריינא
Yiddish for pure or clean.

RAZI, RAZIA, RAZIELLA
רזי, רזיה, רזאלה
Aramaic for secret. Razili means my secret.

REBECCA, REBEKAH, RIVKA רבקה
Beautiful, or to tie or bind. The wife of Isaac, mother of Jacob and Esau, Rebecca was the strong-willed matriarch who masterminded Jacob's deception of his father to gain the family blessing. Nicknames include Becky and Rikki.

REGINA
Sephardic name meaning queen. The Hebrew version is Malkah.

RIMONA רמונה
Pomegranate.

RINA רנה
Joy or song. Renana, Renanit are variations.

RIVA ריבה
Young girl, also a diminutive of Rebecca.
RONA, RONI, RONIT, RONIA
רנה, רוני, רונית, רוניה
Joy or song.

ROSE, ROSA רוזה
The translation from the popular Hebrew name Shoshana. Rose has been a popular name in many languages, including English, Yiddish, Ladino, and Hebrew. (See Raisel, Susan, Varda, Vered.)

Rose Schneiderman (1882–1972) was an American labor organizer and president of the Women's Trade Union League from 1918 to 1949.

RUTH רות
Friendship. The daughter-in-law of Naomi, Ruth chose to stay with Naomi and the Jewish people after the death of her husband. Ruth is considered the model of the righteous convert to Judaism. She is the ancestor of David, from whose line—says the tradition—will come the Messiah.

S   שׁ

SAGIT   שגית
Sublime.

SAMANTHA
Samantha is often given in memory of a Samuel, although there is no connection between the two names. It is not a Hebrew name at all.

SARA, SARAH   שרה
Princess. Sarah is the first Jewish woman. The wife of Abraham, she gave birth to Isaac at the age of ninety. She was known for her beauty, and her hospitality. Nicknames include: Sari, Sarene, Sarina, Sarit. Yiddish versions include: Sorale, Soralie. Sadie, once a common Jewish-American variation, is making a comeback in the United States.

SASHA
Variation on Alexandra, used as a proper name in America.

SERAFINA   שרפינה
To burn. From the same root as the biblical seraphim, angels surrounding God's throne.

SHALVIA, SYLVIA   שלויה
Peace, tranquillity.

SHARON   שרון
A variety of rose in Israel. King Solomon sang of the roses of Sharon.

SHAYNA, SHAINE   שיינא
Yiddish for beautiful.

SHELI, SHELLI   שלי
Mine.

SHIFRA   שפרה
Beautiful. Shifra the midwife,
and her colleague Puah, disobeyed Pharaoh's order to kill all
male Hebrews at birth. A popular Israeli name.

SHIRA, SHIRI   שירה, שירי
Song. My song.

SHLOMIT   שלומית
Peaceful.

SHLOMIYA   שלומיה
Peace.

SHOSHANA   שושנה
A lily or a rose.

SHULAMIT   שולמית
Peace. Shula is a nickname.

SIDRA, SIDRAH   סדרה
Torah portion.

SIMA   סימה
Aramaic for gift.

SIMCHA   שמחה
Joy.

SIMONA, SIMONE   סימונה
To hear. The feminine of
Simon, Simeon.

SIVANA   סיונה
Ninth month of the year.

SIVIA, SIVYA, TZIVIA   צביה
Deer.

STAV   סתו
Autumn

T ט

TAL, TALIA, TALYA, TALI
טל, טליה, טלי
Dew.

TALMA תלמה
Hill.

TAMAR, TAMARA תמר, תמרה
Date palm. Also, righteous and
graceful. A Yiddish variation is
Tema.

TEMIMA תמימה
Innocent.

TIFERET תפארת
Beautiful.

TIKVA תקוה
Hope.

TIRA טירה
Castle.

TIRZA תרצה
Cypress, also desirable. In the
Bible, Tirza was the capital of
Samaria.

TORI תורי
My turtledove.

TOVA טובה
Good one. Often changed to
Toby in English.

TZAFRIRA צפרירה
Morning breeze.

107

TZIPORA צפורה
Little bird. Moses' wife. Also spelled Zipporah. Tzipi is a common nickname.

TZIPOREN צפורן
Carnation.

TZURIA צוריה
Steadfast.

U   א

URIT   אורית
Light.

V

VARDA   ורדה
Rose.

VERED   ורד
Rose.

VIDA, VITA   וידה
Sephardic name meaning life. The equivalent of Eve, or the Hebrew Chaya.

Y   𝔂

YAEL, YAELA, YAALIT
יעל, יעלה, יעלית
God is willing. Feminine version of Yoel or Joel.

YAFFA   יפה
Beautiful. And the name of an Israeli city.

YAFIT   יפית
Beautiful.

YAKIRA   יקירה
Precious.

YARDENA   ירדנה
River Jordan.

YARKONA   ירקונה
Green. Also, a golden green bird found in southern Israel and a river in northern Israel.

YEDIDA   ידידה
Friend, beloved. The mother of Josiah a king of Judah.

YEHIELA   יחיאלה
May God live.

YEIRA   יאירה
Light.

YEMIMA   ימימה
Dove. A daughter of Job. Jemima in English.

YISRAELA   ישראלה
Israeli or Jew.

YOCHEVED   יוכבד
God is glorious. An unsung matriarch, Yocheved, the wife

111

of Amram, was the mother of
Moses, Aaron, and Miriam.

YONA, YONINA, YONIT   ,יונה
יונינה, יונית
Dove.

Z ᵉᵗᵇᵧ ז

ZAHARA, ZEHARI   זהרה, זהרי
Brightness.

ZAHAVA, ZAHAVI, ZEHAVIT
      זהבה, זהבי, זהבית
Golden.

ZARA, ZORA   זרה
Variations on Sarah. Also, Zora
is Arabic for dawn.

ZEVA   זאבה
Wolf.

ZIKIT   זיקית
Longing.

ZILLA, TZILA   צילה
Shadow.

ZIONA   ציונה
Excellent.

ZIVA, ZIVIT   זיוה, זיוית
Splendor, radiant.

ZIVANIT   זיונית
Mayflower.

Glossary

ARAMAIC   Semitic language closely related to Hebrew, the lingua franca of the Middle East. The Talmud was written in Aramaic.

ASHKENAZIC   Jews and Jewish culture of Eastern and Central Europe.

HASIDISM   Eighteenth-century mystical revival movement that stressed God's immanence in the world. The doctrine of *simcha*, or joy, was taught as a way of communing with God.

MENSCH   Person. An honorable, decent person.

MIDRASH   Imaginative exposition of or stories based upon holy scriptures. Also, a body of literature of the same name.

MISHNA   The first part of the Talmud, comprised of six "orders" of laws regarding everything from agriculture to marriage.

MOHEL   Someone who is trained in the rituals and procedures of circumcision, *brit milah*.

SABRA   Native-born Israeli.

SEPHARDIC   Jews and Jewish culture of Spain and the Mediterranean.

TALMUD   Collection of rabbinic thought and laws from 200 B.C.E. to 500 C.E.

YICHUS   Family status. Pride in family member's achievements.

YIDDISH   Language spoken by Ashkenazic Jews, a combination of early German and Hebrew.

YIDDISHKEIT   Jewishness, Jewish culture.

Notes

1. In the past, and in many Orthodox communities today, only the father's name is affixed; thus *Michael bar Moshe*, or *Hanna bat Chaim*. In the last twenty years or so, however, liberal Jewish practice has been to include both parents' Hebrew names.

2. Nathan Gottlieb, *A Jewish Child is Born*. (New York: Bloch Publishing Co., 1960) p. 111.

3. Alfred Kolatch, *The Name Dictionary*. (Middle Village, N.Y., Jonathan David Publishers, 1967) p. xi.

4. Benzion C. Kaganoff, *A Dictionary of Jewish Names and Their History*. (New York: Schocken Books, 1977) p. 49.

5. Kaganoff. p. 53.

6. Rabbi Herbert C. Dobrinski, *A Treasury of Sephardic Laws and Customs* (New York and Hoboken, N.J.: Yeshiva University & Ktav, 1986) p. 4.

7. Dobrinski, p. 61.

8. Dobrinski, p. 4.

9. Nesvisky, Matthew, "There's Miki, Riki, Tiki, Suki, Shuli, Tzippi, Tzuri, Uri, and Nuri," *Moment Magazine*, Vol. 9. #8, September 1984/Elul 5744, pp 47–51.

10. Nesvisky, p. 50.